WORK

For

I Thought It Was Just Me (but it isn't)

Making the Journey from "What Will People Think?" to "I Am Enough"

[A Comprehensive Guide To implementing

Brené Brown's Book]

Dunne Press

This workbook is intended to be used as a companion to the book. While it can be utilized independently, it is designed to enhance the reader's experience and understanding of the concepts presented in the book. This workbook is not intended to replace or serve as a substitute for the original book.

Table of Content

How To Use This Workbook

Welcome to the companion workbook for **I Thought It Was Just Me (but it isn't): Making the Journey from "What Will People Think?" to "I Am Enough"** by Brené Brown. This workbook is designed to help you dive deeper into the content of the original book and apply its principles to your life. Here's how to use this book:

Overview

The workbook starts with a general summary of the original book, which provides an overview of the key themes and concepts.

Chapter Sections

Each chapter in the workbook includes the following sections:

- Summary: A brief summary of the chapter's content.
- Key Lessons: A list of the key lessons from the chapter.
- Self-Reflection Questions: A list of questions designed to help you reflect on the chapter's content and apply it to your life.
- Action Steps: A list of practical steps you can take to apply the chapter's content to your life.

Learning Review Questions

At the end of the workbook, there is a section of Learning Review questions. These questions are designed to help you review and reinforce the key concepts from the book. You can use these questions to test your understanding of the material and identify areas where you may need to review or study further.

To get the most out of this workbook, we recommend the following:

- Read the overview of the original book before starting the workbook.
- Read each chapter of the workbook carefully, taking notes as needed.
- Complete the self-reflection questions for each chapter, taking time to reflect on your answers.
- Use the action steps to apply the chapter's content to your life.
- Review the Learning Review questions at the end of the workbook to reinforce your understanding of the material.

Overview

"I Thought It Was Just Me (but it isn't): Making the Journey from 'What Will People Think?' to 'I Am Enough" is a book authored by Brené Brown, a research professor and author recognized for her work on vulnerability, shame, and resilience. The book analyzes the issue of shame and its influence on women, giving insights and techniques to overcome shame and build self-acceptance.

The book starts by presenting the notion of shame and its persistent influence in our lives. Brown describes shame as the very painful sense of knowing that we are imperfect, insufficient, and undeserving of love and belonging. She thinks that shame is universal and affects everyone from all walks of life, but women tend to feel it differently owing to social expectations, cultural norms, and gender roles.

Throughout the book, Brown provides personal tales, scientific data, and the lives of many women she has interviewed to highlight the complicated nature of shame. She demonstrates how guilt typically arises from cultural demands to satisfy unattainable ideals of beauty, parenting, relationships, and career. Brown highlights the significance of identifying shame and comprehending its influence on our lives in order to break free from its grasp.

The author stresses the damaging impacts of shame, including alienation from ourselves and others, and presents solutions for fostering empathy, bravery, and resilience. She urges readers to cultivate self-compassion, accept vulnerability, and form supportive relationships. Brown highlights the significance of owning our story, embracing mistakes, and practicing self-love.

The book also investigates the link between shame and other feelings, such as remorse, embarrassment, and humiliation. Brown demonstrates how recognizing the nuances between these emotions may help people handle guilt more successfully and create better coping skills.

The book also addresses the societal and cultural reasons that promote shame, including the impact of media, social expectations, and gender roles. Brown presents incisive analysis and invites readers to fight and modify the societal conventions that lead to shame and restrict women's ability to accept themselves.

Overall, the book is a riveting and motivating book that shines light on the widespread nature of shame and gives practical strategies to overcome it. Brené Brown's research, personal anecdotes, and compassionate attitude make this book a useful resource for anybody trying to foster self-acceptance, resilience, and a more genuine and happy life.

Understanding Shame

Summary

Brené Brown digs into the notion of shame and its enormous influence on our lives. She describes shame as the terrible sensation of being worthless and imperfect, stressing its widespread existence in our culture. Brown analyzes the varied types of shame experienced by women, impacted by society's expectations and cultural conventions. She highlights the necessity of identifying shame, understanding its impacts, and finding solutions to overcome it.

Key Lessons

- Shame is a universal feeling that impacts people from all walks of life.
- Shame stems from society's expectations and cultural conventions, especially for women.
- Shame is a highly unpleasant sense of being imperfect and worthless.
- Recognizing and comprehending shame is vital for breaking free from its control.
- Shame disconnects us from ourselves and others, preventing true interactions.
- Developing empathy, bravery, and resilience may help overcome shame.

Self-Reflection Questions

In what ways have cultural expectations affected your experience of shame?

_____

_____

_____

_____

_____

_____

_____

_____

_____

_____

_____

_____

_____

How does shame express itself in your life, and how does it affect your relationships?

_____

_____

_____

_____

_____

_____

_____

_____

_____

_____

_____

_____

Are there certain triggers or events that constantly generate emotions of shame?

_____

_____

_____

_____

_____

_____

_____

_____

_____

_____

_____

_____

What tactics have you employed in the past to deal with shame, and how helpful have they been?

_____

_____

_____

_____

_____

_____

_____

_____

_____

_____

_____

_____

_____

How do you define self-worth, and how has shame changed your perspective on it?

_____

_____

_____

_____

_____

_____

_____

_____

_____

_____

_____

_____

_____

_____

Can you recall situations when you have projected your own guilt onto others?

_____

_____

_____

_____

_____

_____

_____

_____

_____

_____

_____

Action Steps

- Reflect on your personal experiences with shame and notice any repeating patterns or triggers.
- Seek help from trustworthy friends or experts to investigate and confront your shame.
- Challenge social expectations and cultural conventions that lead to shame.
- Practice self-compassion by accepting your merit despite your shortcomings.
- Cultivate empathy by actively listening to people and attempting to understand their perspectives.
- Develop resilience by accepting vulnerability and taking chances in a secure and supportive setting.
- Share your story with others, establishing relationships and ending the cycle of shame.

Shame Resilience and the Power of Empathy

Summary

The author dives into the value of empathy in establishing resilience against shame. In this chapter, Brené Brown investigates the notion of shame resilience and its link to empathy. She highlights the value of empathy in fighting guilt and creating resilience. Brown adds that empathy entails perceiving and comprehending the feelings of others without judgment or comparison.

Key Lessons

- Empathy is vital in establishing resistance against shame.
- Empathy entails noticing and understanding the feelings of others without judgment.
- Empathy develops connection and facilitates healing.
- Shame and empathy are interrelated, because empathy may mitigate the isolating consequences of shame.
- Cultivating empathy takes practice in active listening, perspective-taking, and genuine inquiry.
- Empathy entails leaving aside one's own experiences and actually stepping into the shoes of another person.
- Empathy is a talent that can be learned and improved through practice and purpose.

Self-Reflection Questions

How do you now exhibit empathy towards others when they disclose their weaknesses or struggles?

_____

_____

_____

_____

_____

_____

_____

_____

_____

_____

_____

_____

_____

Do you tend to evaluate or compare others' experiences and emotions? How may this affect your capacity to connect with them on a deeper level?

_____

_____

_____

_____

_____

_____

_____

_____

_____

_____

_____

_____

Are there instances when you find it tough to show empathy? What could be the fundamental causes behind this difficulty?

_____

_____

_____

_____

_____

_____

_____

_____

_____

_____

_____

_____

Reflect on a recent incident when you felt humiliated. How may empathy have benefited you in that situation?

_____

_____

_____

_____

_____

_____

_____

_____

_____

_____

_____

_____

How can you create a better feeling of curiosity and genuine interest in others' experiences and emotions?

_____

_____

_____

_____

_____

_____

_____

_____

_____

_____

_____

_____

What hurdles or prejudices can hamper your capacity to exercise empathy effectively?

_____

_____

_____

_____

_____

_____

_____

_____

_____

_____

_____

_____

Action Steps

- Practice active listening in interactions, concentrating on completely understanding and validating the feelings communicated by others.
- Engage in perspective-taking tasks to build a greater awareness of other life situations.
- Challenge any temptation to evaluate or compare when someone exposes their weaknesses or challenges.
- Prioritize providing safe and non-judgmental settings for open and honest talks.
- Set aside your own experiences and preconceptions to truly immerse yourself in the viewpoints of others.
- Seek chances to learn about diverse cultures, backgrounds, and experiences to extend your empathy.
- Make a commitment to consistently participate in empathy-building activities, such as volunteering, participating in community conversations, or reading other viewpoints.

The First Element: Recognizing Shame and Understanding Our Triggers

Summary

Brown focuses on the first aspect of conquering shame: identifying shame and understanding our triggers. She highlights the necessity of being aware of shame in our lives and addressing the exact events, experiences, or ideas that elicit shame reactions. Brown emphasizes that identifying shame is the first step towards creating resilience and modifying our relationship with shame.

Key Lessons

- Shame is typically a natural and deeply entrenched emotional reaction to perceived defects or weaknesses.
- Recognizing shame takes self-awareness and paying attention to the physical, emotional, and behavioral markers that indicate its existence.
- Shame triggers may be varied and unique to each individual, affected by personal experience, cultural expectations, and social conventions.
- Understanding our shame triggers helps us see patterns, create connections, and get insight into our emotional reactions.
- Shame may emerge as a spiral of negative self-talk and self-criticism, leading to separation and isolation.

24

Self-Reflection Questions

What bodily feelings or emotions do you experience when you're in a shame-triggering situation?

_____

_____

_____

_____

_____

_____

_____

_____

_____

_____

_____

_____

Are there repeating themes or patterns in the incidents that generate guilt in your life?

_____

_____

_____

_____

_____

_____

_____

_____

_____

_____

_____

_____

_____

How do social expectations and cultural standards impact your feeling of shame?

_____

_____

_____

_____

_____

_____

_____

_____

_____

_____

_____

_____

How do you generally react to shame? Do you retreat, get defensive, or indulge in self-criticism?

_____

_____

_____

_____

_____

_____

_____

_____

_____

_____

_____

_____

Are there certain memories or experiences from your history that frequently provoke emotions of shame?

_____

_____

_____

_____

_____

_____

_____

_____

_____

_____

_____

_____

How can recognizing and addressing shame experiences effect your capacity to connect with others?

_____

_____

_____

_____

_____

_____

_____

_____

_____

_____

_____

_____

Action Steps

- Practice mindfulness and self-awareness to notice physical, emotional, and behavioral indicators that indicate the existence of shame.
- Keep a notebook or record of shame-triggering circumstances to detect trends and acquire deeper understanding into your triggers.
- Seek help from trustworthy friends or experts who can give empathy and understanding while addressing shame.
- Challenge social norms and cultural expectations that lead to shame by challenging their validity and influence on your well-being.
- Develop a language to describe and define shame experiences, allowing for more self-expression and connection with others.
- Cultivate self-compassion via self-talk, affirmations, and accepting faults as part of the human experience.
- Practice vulnerability by sharing your shame experiences with trustworthy people or in supportive groups to encourage healing and resilience.

The Second Element: Practicing Critical Awareness

Summary

In this chapter, Brown addresses the notion of critical awareness and its role in overcoming shame and creating resilience. Brown dives into the necessity of cultivating critical awareness as a tool to question and overcome guilt. Brown adds that critical awareness requires examining and assessing the social expectations and cultural norms that lead to shame.

Key Lessons

- By understanding the social expectations and cultural ideas that lead to shame, people may begin to confront and modify the narratives that undermine their self-worth.
- Bringing shame out into the open and addressing it freely with others may decrease its power and provide chances for healing and progress.
- Recognize the events, people, or surroundings that tend to cause shame and intentionally work towards developing resilience and self-compassion in such times.

- Understanding the difference between shame (feeling intrinsically imperfect) and guilt (feeling sorrow for particular acts) assists in creating a healthy emotional reaction to errors and failures.
- Cultivate self-kindness, understanding, and acceptance, particularly while experiencing shame-inducing circumstances. Treat yourself with the same kindness you would show a loved one.
- Question the beauty standards, gender roles, and other cultural expectations that lead to shame and attempt to reframe them on your own terms.
- Engage with a supportive community or seek professional assistance to manage shame and build critical awareness. Sharing experiences with others may create connection, empathy, and healing.

Self-Reflection Questions

How do social expectations and cultural standards contribute to the sense of shame in your life?

_____

_____

_____

_____

_____

_____

_____

_____

_____

_____

_____

_____

Are there certain events or people who tend to provoke emotions of shame in you? How can you create resilience and self-compassion in such moments?

_____

_____

_____

_____

_____

_____

_____

_____

_____

_____

_____

What messages have you absorbed about your worthiness? How can you confront and reinterpret those beliefs?

_____

_____

_____

_____

_____

_____

_____

_____

_____

_____

_____

_____

_____

How do you generally react to shame? Are there additional useful ways you can approach and manage shame-inducing experiences?

_____

_____

_____

_____

_____

_____

_____

_____

_____

_____

_____

_____

How do you discern between shame and guilt? How might recognizing this difference help you handle these emotions more effectively?

_____

_____

_____

_____

_____

_____

_____

_____

_____

_____

_____

_____

Action Steps

- Take time to evaluate the cultural messages and social expectations that lead to shame in your life.
- Develop skills to react to events or people that tend to provoke shame in healthier and more self-compassionate ways.
- Find safe venues and supportive groups to explore and share your shame experiences freely.
- Cultivate a daily self-compassion practice, such as affirmations, writing, or meditation, to cultivate acceptance and love towards oneself.
- Identify and question cultural norms and expectations that lead to shame and reframe them based on your own values and beliefs.
- Consider participating in counseling or obtaining direction from a mental health expert to negotiate shame and build critical awareness.
- Surround yourself with sensitive and understanding people who can help you in your journey towards self-acceptance and resilience.

The Third Element: Reaching Out

Summary

Brown addresses the necessity of reaching out to others as a method of healing shame and fostering resilience. She underlines that shame flourishes in isolation and that connection and empathy are vital to loosening its grasp on our lives. Brown provides research data and personal tales to highlight how reaching out and developing supportive connections may contribute to our feelings of self-worth and belonging.

Key Lessons

- Shame flourishes in isolation: Keeping our challenges and weaknesses to ourselves amplifies feelings of shame.
- Connection is essential: Building real and supportive connections is vital for healing shame and creating resilience.
- Empathy combats shame: Receiving and providing empathy helps us connect with people and understand we are not alone in our experiences.
- Vulnerability in sharing: Sharing our shame stories with trustworthy people may be transformational and lead to deeper relationships.
- Boundaries are necessary: Establishing healthy boundaries shields us from shame triggers and enables true interactions.

Self-Reflection Questions

How comfortable are you with reaching out to others for help during hard times?

_____

_____

_____

_____

_____

_____

_____

_____

_____

_____

_____

What fears or beliefs restrict you from seeking connection and exposing your vulnerabilities?

_____

_____

_____

_____

_____

_____

_____

_____

_____

_____

_____

_____

_____

How can you build empathy and compassion for others' shame experiences?

_____

_____

_____

_____

_____

_____

_____

_____

_____

_____

_____

_____

What limits do you need to create to protect yourself while still building meaningful connections?

_____

_____

_____

_____

_____

_____

_____

_____

_____

_____

_____

_____

How can you practice self-compassion and show yourself kindness while you're experiencing shame?

_____

_____

_____

_____

_____

_____

_____

_____

_____

_____

_____

_____

_____

Who are the individuals in your life with whom you can truly share your shame stories?

_____

_____

_____

_____

_____

_____

_____

_____

_____

_____

_____

Action Steps

- Identify at least one person you trust and feel secure with, and reach out to them to share a sensitive experience.
- Practice active listening and empathy by completely engaging with others' tales and experiences without judgment.
- Set limits in your relationships to preserve your emotional well-being while retaining meaningful connections.
- Seek out support groups, counseling, or online forums where you may connect with people who have similar experiences.
- Embrace self-compassion by speaking lovingly to yourself and realizing that everyone suffers from shame.
- Make a commitment to routinely check in with friends or loved ones, giving assistance and being open to receiving it.
- Challenge any ideas or anxieties that restrict your capacity to reach out and actively focus on building a mentality of connection and vulnerability.

The Fourth Element: Speaking Shame

Summary

The author addresses the value of voicing shame as a form of healing and connection. She underlines the value of sharing our shame stories with empathic and trustworthy people to break away from the isolating grasp of shame. Brown adds that by addressing shame, we not only reduce its load but also generate a feeling of belonging and empathy.

Key Lessons

- Speaking out against shame is a vital step in removing its grip on our lives.
- Sharing our shame stories with empathic listeners creates connection and belonging.
- Vulnerability is essential to honestly voicing shame.
- Finding trustworthy people who can carry our shame stories is vital.
- The act of admitting shame dispels the concealment and power that shame has.
- Speaking out against shame helps to question and modify the societal conventions that perpetuate it.
- Speaking out of shame opens the path to healing and self-acceptance.

Self-Reflection Questions

Have you ever addressed your shame stories with someone you trust? How did it make you feel?

_____

_____

_____

_____

_____

_____

_____

_____

_____

_____

_____

_____

What anxieties or doubts do you have about expressing your shame to others?

_____

_____

_____

_____

_____

_____

_____

_____

_____

_____

_____

_____

_____

Do you feel that voicing shame may promote a sense of connection and belonging? Why or why not?

_____

_____

_____

_____

_____

_____

_____

_____

_____

_____

_____

_____

Are there certain people in your life that you deem trustworthy enough to hold your shame stories?

_____

_____

_____

_____

_____

_____

_____

_____

_____

_____

_____

_____

How do you believe addressing shame may help your personal development and self-acceptance?

_____

_____

_____

_____

_____

_____

_____

_____

_____

_____

_____

_____

In what ways may addressing shame confront and modify the societal norms that sustain shame?

_____

_____

_____

_____

_____

_____

_____

_____

_____

_____

_____

_____

Action Steps

- Identify at least one trustworthy person with whom you feel comfortable discussing your shame tales.
- Reflect on and write down your shame tales, enabling yourself to fully accept and comprehend them.
- Practice vulnerability by progressively sharing your shame stories with someone you trust.
- Seek out support groups or therapy sessions that provide a secure environment for voicing shame and connecting with others.
- Challenge the culture of shame by freely addressing your experiences and encouraging others to do the same.
- Engage in self-compassion activities to create a more tolerant attitude towards your own shame experiences.
- Make a commitment to listen empathetically and without judgment when people share their shame stories, providing a supportive and non-judgmental atmosphere.

Practicing Courage in a Culture of Fear

Summary

Brené Brown goes into the issue of exercising bravery in a society driven by fear. She analyzes how fear impacts our lives, stifles vulnerability, and promotes shame. Brown urges readers to tackle their concerns and build resilience by embracing bravery.

Key Lessons

- Fear is strongly engrained in our culture and impacts numerous facets of our lives, frequently leading to guilt and alienation.
- To build bravery, one must accept vulnerability and be prepared to take emotional risks.
- Allowing fear to govern us hampers personal development and hinders our capacity to live truthfully.
- Comparing ourselves to others deepens dread and keeps us caught in a cycle of self-doubt and guilt.
- Developing shame resilience is vital to negotiating fear and embracing bravery. It entails identifying shame, exercising empathy, and building self-compassion.
- Empathy and compassion are vital skills for breaking free from fear and creating relationships with others.
- By exercising courage, we inspire people around us and create a ripple effect of bravery and sincerity.

Self-Reflection Questions

How does fear affect your desire to be vulnerable?

_____

_____

_____

_____

_____

_____

_____

_____

_____

_____

_____

_____

In what areas of your life do you perceive fear impeding your development and authenticity?

_____

_____

_____

_____

_____

_____

_____

_____

_____

_____

_____

_____

How can comparing yourself to others contribute to your worries and feelings of inadequacy?

_____

_____

_____

_____

_____

_____

_____

_____

_____

_____

_____

_____

What measures can you take to improve resilience in the face of guilt and fear?

_____

_____

_____

_____

_____

_____

_____

_____

_____

_____

_____

_____

How can you create empathy and compassion towards yourself and others to overcome fear?

_____

_____

_____

_____

_____

_____

_____

_____

_____

_____

_____

_____

Think about a moment when you observed someone's daring deed. How did it inspire you, and how can you implement that inspiration into your own life?

Action Steps

- Identify one area of your life where fear is holding you back, and make a commitment to take a tiny step towards tackling that fear.
- Discuss your concerns and anxieties with a trustworthy friend or family member and asking for their support.
- Challenge the tendency toward comparison by concentrating on your own success and improvement rather than comparing yourself to others.
- Engage in daily activities of self-compassion, such as writing in a gratitude diary or practicing mindfulness meditation.
- Seek out opportunities to empathize with others and exhibit compassion, both in your personal relationships and in your community.
- Share your heroic deeds and vulnerabilities with others, sharing your experiences to inspire and motivate people around you.
- Continually reflect on your road towards bravery and be open to altering your actions and thoughts as required. Remember that bravery is a lifetime exercise.

Practicing Compassion in a Culture of Blame

Summary

The author addresses the significance of practicing compassion in a society that frequently resorts to blaming. She underlines the damaging nature of blame and its influence on people and relationships. Brown highlights the need for empathy and understanding to fight the culture of blame and develop stronger relationships.

Key Lessons

- Blaming ourselves or others just reinforces the cycle of shame and hampers development and healing.
- Understanding others' viewpoints and experiences helps us exhibit compassion and connect on a deeper level.
- Realizing that everyone makes errors and endures hardships helps us approach others with empathy and understanding.
- Choosing empathy and compassion over blame helps us develop stronger relationships and encourage personal growth.
- Examining our own inclinations to blame might help us break away from the culture of blame and create personal development.

Self-Reflection Questions

In what instances do you find yourself reverting to blaming rather than exercising compassion?

_____

_____

_____

_____

_____

_____

_____

_____

_____

_____

_____

_____

How does blaming affect your relationships with others and with yourself?

_____

_____

_____

_____

_____

_____

_____

_____

_____

_____

_____

What cultural or social elements contribute to a culture of blame in your life?

_____

_____

_____

_____

_____

_____

_____

_____

_____

_____

_____

_____

How can you build a greater awareness of others'
experiences and viewpoints to encourage compassion?

_____

_____

_____

_____

_____

_____

_____

_____

_____

_____

_____

_____

_____

Are there certain triggers or patterns that encourage you to engage in blame? How do you break away from these patterns?

_____

_____

_____

_____

_____

_____

_____

_____

_____

_____

_____

_____

_____

What role does vulnerability play in developing compassion and breaking free from blame?

_____

_____

_____

_____

_____

_____

_____

_____

_____

_____

_____

_____

Action Steps

- Treat yourself with care and empathy, acknowledging that everyone makes errors.
- Take the time to listen and sympathize with people, even when you disagree or feel provoked.
- Question the tales and ideas that lead to blame and seek other viewpoints.
- Engage in activities that help you build empathy, such as reading diverse literature or participating in meaningful discussions.
- Foster places where people may express themselves without fear of condemnation or judgment.
- Identify events or actions that are likely to push you toward blaming and learn alternate responses.
- Actively encourage compassion and understanding in your contacts with others, modeling the conduct you desire to see in the world.

Practicing Connection in a Culture of Disconnection

Summary

Brown addresses the value of connection in a world that fosters separation. She underlines the harmful impacts of social pressure and underscores the necessity for true personal connection and empathy. Brown urges readers to learn the skills required to promote connection, both with oneself and with others, as a strategy to overcome shame and build resilience.

Key Lessons

- Living in a society of separation may heighten emotions of shame and inadequacy.
- By understanding and acknowledging the perspectives of others, we create a supportive and empathetic atmosphere.
- Being open and real in our relationships helps develop deeper connections, as it enables people to see and relate to our actual selves.
- Establishing and maintaining appropriate boundaries is crucial for establishing meaningful friendships.
- Building and sustaining relationships requires continual work and attention.

Self-Reflection Questions

How does living in a culture of isolation affect your feelings of self-worth and shame?

_____

_____

_____

_____

_____

_____

_____

_____

_____

_____

_____

_____

In what ways have you experienced the positive influence of true human connection?

_____

_____

_____

_____

_____

_____

_____

_____

_____

_____

_____

_____

_____

How can you create empathy in your relationships with others?

_____

_____

_____

_____

_____

_____

_____

_____

_____

_____

_____

_____

Are you comfortable being vulnerable and real in your relationships? If not, what impediments are keeping you from doing so?

_____

_____

_____

_____

_____

_____

_____

_____

_____

_____

_____

Do you have clear boundaries in your relationships? How can you encourage them to maintain healthy connections?

_____

_____

_____

_____

_____

_____

_____

_____

_____

_____

_____

_____

_____

Are you practicing self-compassion? How can you be nicer and more understanding toward yourself?

_____

_____

_____

_____

_____

_____

_____

_____

_____

_____

_____

_____

_____

Action Steps

- Reach out to someone you trust and have a discussion about vulnerability and connection.
- Practice active listening and empathy in your dealings with others, aiming to genuinely comprehend their experiences and feelings.
- Reflect on your present connections and decide whether any boundaries need to be set or enforced.
- Engage in activities that develop authenticity, such as writing or attending a support group where you can express your experiences honestly.
- Prioritize self-care and self-compassion by implementing daily routines that encourage self-acceptance and kindness.
- Seek chances to engage with like-minded people or groups that correspond with your beliefs and interests.
- Make a commitment to constantly invest in your connections by setting aside specific time for fostering relationships and practicing vulnerability.

Creating a Culture of Connection

Summary

In this chapter, the author examines the necessity of fostering a culture of connection. She examines the influence of guilt on relationships and presents techniques for creating meaningful connections and building a supportive community.

Key Lessons

- To develop true friendships, we must be willing to show up truthfully, disclose our weaknesses, and be open to accepting help.
- Empathy, the capacity to understand and share the emotions of others, is a critical factor in developing a culture of connection
- Shame loses strength when it is brought into the light. By sharing our stories and experiences, we tear down the barriers of shame and make room for connection and healing.
- Honest and honest dialogues help bridge the gap between individuals and develop understanding.
- Boundaries are crucial for good partnerships. They help us determine what is acceptable and what is not, ensuring that we prioritize our personal well-being while still being connected to others.

Self-Reflection Questions

How eager are you to be vulnerable and reveal your genuine self to others?

_____

_____

_____

_____

_____

_____

_____

_____

_____

_____

_____

_____

Do you actively listen and demonstrate empathy towards others' experiences and emotions?

_____

_____

_____

_____

_____

_____

_____

_____

_____

_____

_____

In what ways do you contribute to building a culture of connectedness in your personal and professional relationships?

_____

_____

_____

_____

_____

_____

_____

_____

_____

_____

_____

_____

How comfortable are you with participating in daring talks that handle challenging topics?

_____

_____

_____

_____

_____

_____

_____

_____

_____

_____

_____

_____

Are your boundaries obvious and honored in your relationships?

_____

_____

_____

_____

_____

_____

_____

_____

_____

_____

_____

_____

_____

What measures can you take to build a sense of belonging and inclusion in your community?

_____

_____

_____

_____

_____

_____

_____

_____

_____

_____

_____

_____

Action Steps

- Reflect on your own vulnerability and discover places where you can show up truthfully in your relationships.
- Share your own experiences and stories, particularly those relating to shame, to create an atmosphere where others feel comfortable doing the same.
- Initiate daring dialogues by discussing difficult subjects with kindness and respect.
- Evaluate your limits and express them effectively to create healthy and balanced relationships.
- Seek ways to engage with various people and make an effort to comprehend their stories.
- Prioritize self-compassion by treating yourself with love, accepting shortcomings, and exercising self-care while cultivating relationships with others.

Learning Review Questions

Did you achieve your intended goals or objectives as described at the start of this workbook? Why or why not?

_____

_____

_____

_____

_____

_____

_____

_____

_____

_____

_____

_____

_____

In reflecting on your progress throughout the workbook, what were the key strengths you displayed in your learning and personal growth?

_____

_____

_____

_____

_____

_____

_____

_____

_____

_____

_____

_____

_____

_____

What were the most difficult sections or subjects in this workbook for you? How did you overcome such difficulties?

_____

_____

_____

_____

_____

_____

_____

_____

_____

_____

_____

_____

_____

_____

How did this worksheet help you grasp the subject? Did it live up to your expectations in terms of insightful insights and practical application?

_____

_____

_____

_____

_____

_____

_____

_____

_____

_____

_____

_____

_____

_____

Think about the chapter questions and action tasks provided in this worksheet. Which ones did you find most useful, and why? How did you incorporate them into your regular life or routine?

_____

_____

_____

_____

_____

_____

_____

_____

_____

_____

_____

_____

_____

_____

In reflecting on your experience with this workbook, what changes or improvements have you noticed in yourself? How has your perspective, mentality, or conduct changed?

_____

_____

_____

_____

_____

_____

_____

_____

_____

_____

_____

_____

_____

_____

_____

How would you grade the arrangement and structure of this workbook? Was it simple to follow and did it flow logically from one section to the next?

_____

_____

_____

_____

_____

_____

_____

_____

_____

_____

_____

_____

Overall, how would you rate the usefulness of this workbook in assisting you to attain your personal or learning goals? What specific factors contributed to or detracted from its effectiveness?

_____

_____

_____

_____

_____

_____

_____

_____

_____

_____

_____

_____

_____

_____

Made in United States
Troutdale, OR
11/04/2023

14281136R00056